C000121361

BALINESE
Architecture

JULIAN DAVISON
& BRUCE GRANQUIST

PERIPLUS

Copyright © 1999 Periplus Editions (HK) Ltd.

Printed in Singapore
ISBN 962-593-194-5

Publisher: Eric M. Oey
Text: Julian Davison
Illustrations: Bruce Granquist, Mubinas Hanafi,
Nengah Enu and Julian Davison
Production: Violet Wong & Agnes Tan

Distributors
Indonesia:
PT Wira Mandala Pustaka
(Java Books–Indonesia)
Jalan Kelapa Gading Kirana
Blok A14 No. 17
Jakarta 14240

Asia Pacific:
Berkeley Books Pte. Ltd.
5 Little Road #08-01, Singapore 536983

North America, Latin America and Europe:
Tuttle Publishing, Distribution Center
Airport Industrial Park, 364 Innovation Drive
North Clarendon, VT 05759-9436

Japan:
Tuttle Publishing, RK Building 2nd Floor
2-13-10 Shimo-Meguro,
Meguro-Ku, Tokyo 153 0064, Japan

Contents

The tripartite division of the universe dovetails with the concept of *Tri Angga*, which assumes that everything in the natural world can be divided into three parts: *nista*, *madya* and *utama*. *Utama*, which in physical terms denotes things that are 'high' or 'above', is identified with mountains and, by extension, the gods who dwell there, heaven and the ancestors, and all that is pure or sacred. *Nista*, on the other hand, denotes things that are 'low' or 'below', which includes the sea and any malevolent spirits, hell and the dead, the impure and the profane. Man occupies the middle ground of *madya*, the mundane world of everyday existence, a kind of cosmological hinterland that stretches from the seashore to the foothills of the central mountain range. The human body can be similarly divided into three parts—head, torso and feet—and this tripartite scheme of things extends to embrace all aspects of creation, including the things that man himself creates. Even the simplest built structure can be separated into three components—a base, the walls or posts, and the roof.

Man, Architecture and the Universe

The archetypal Balinese residence affords a singular way of living in a tropical environment. It comprises a collection of low-profile pavilions set in a walled compound (*pekarangan*), surrounded by ornamental shrubs and fruit trees. Each building is placed on a low plinth and surmounted by a hipped roof clad with clay pantiles or grass thatch. Some structures are open-sided, others are enclosed by masonry walls. Each has a specific function, yet from the humblest *pekarangan* of the common man to the grandest palace (*puri*) of a Balinese prince, the essentials are the same, and reflect an ancient architectural tradition which has its origins, at least in part, in India.

Microcosm and Macrocosm

Balinese architecture is grounded in a metaphysics that presents the universe as an integrated whole, where each part participates in the existence of every other part, and where the microcosm is perceived as a reflection of the macrocosm.

Correct orientation in space, combined with ideas of ritual purity and pollution, are key concepts, providing a cosmological framework for maintaining a harmony between man and the rest of the universe. This view of the world derives from the Hindu idea of a divine cosmic order (dharma), qualified by a much older animistic tradition.

Balinese Hinduism

Indian religious beliefs in Southeast Asia date from the time of Christ when Indian merchants first began to develop trade links with the region.

Balinese Hinduism, however, probably owes more to Javanese influences between the 14th and 16th centuries than it does directly to the Indian subcontinent. This was the era of the mighty East Javanese Majapahit empire (1292–*ca*1525) whose political and cultural influence, at its height, extended over much of the Indonesian archipelago including Bali. The Majapahit dynasty was the last in a long line of Hindu-Buddhist kingdoms in Java which in earlier centuries had been responsible for building the great temple complexes at Borobudur and Prambanan.

By the end of the 15th century, however, the power of Majapahit was on the wane as new Muslim polities were established along the north coast of Java and elsewhere in the archipelago.

The final collapse came in the early years of the 16th century, and led to the removal of the royal court to Bali, where earlier generations of Majapahit colonisers had established themselves as the local elite.

These refugees included artisans, scholars, priests and aristocrats, and they brought with them the religion, manners and artistic conventions of the Javanese court. Over time, these cultural orientations became assimilated as part of the island's unique cultural tradition, giving rise to a

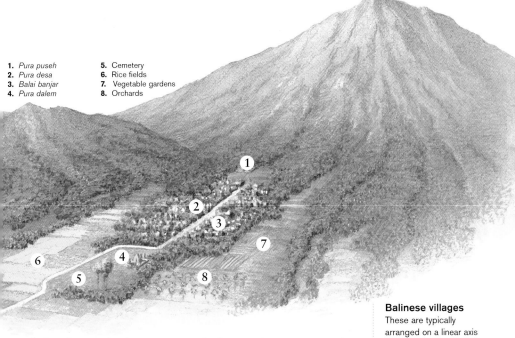

1. *Pura puseh*
2. *Pura desa*
3. *Balai banjar*
4. *Pura dalem*
5. Cemetery
6. Rice fields
7. Vegetable gardens
8. Orchards

singularly Balinese style of Hinduism, shot through with Buddhist influences and infiltrated by indigenous animism.

A Tripartite Universe

Balinese architecture is based on a set of cosmological orientations and ritual considerations, which influence most aspects of life. The Balinese universe comes in multiples of three. The most basic is the division of the cosmos into three domains: the underworld (Buhr), which is the realm of evil and malevolent spirits; the world of human beings (Bhuwah); and the heavens above (Swah), occupied by the gods and deified ancestors.

This cosmological model can be readily mapped on to the local topography where natural divisions occur between the mountains at the centre of the island, the hinterland, and the sea. The mountains are seen as the holiest part of the island—the main places of worship are there—while the sea is cast as an impure region, home to malevolent spirits and evil influences. The coastal plains and foothills, which form an intermediate

realm between the two extremes, is the proper abode of man.

A Sense of Place

For the Balinese, everything has its correct place in the world, with the gods on high, malevolent spirits in the lowest regions, and mankind sandwiched between the two. Proper positioning in relation to the rest of the world is important for maintaining harmonious relations with the rest of the universe, so Balinese architecture is mediated by various spatial orientations to ensure that buildings and their occupants are favourably placed. The two principal directions are *kaja* and *kelod*. *Kaja* is defined as 'towards the mountains', the central mountain range in Bali being identified as the abode of the gods, while *kelod* lies the opposite way, 'towards the sea', a region of great impurity and malign influences, the home of monstrous demons and malevolent spirits. In southern Bali, where most of the population live, *kaja* and *kelod* roughly correspond to north and south respectively, but on the opposite side of the island the reverse is of course the case.

Balinese villages

These are typically arranged on a linear axis between sea and mountains. The temple of origin (*pura puseh*)—dedicated to the community's founders —is at the uphill (*kaja*) end of the village, as befits deified ancestors, while the temple of the dead (*pura dalem*) and the cemetery are at the downhill or seaward (*kelod*) end, reflecting the polluting nature of death.

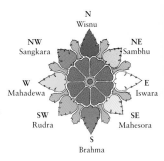

Nawa-sanga

The Balinese compass rose (*nawa-sanga*) stems from the four cardinal directions, their intermediaries and the centre. Each point is linked to a particular deity—Hindu in origin—and has symbolic and ritual associations. This provides a comprehensive framework for the proper orientation of buildings.

5

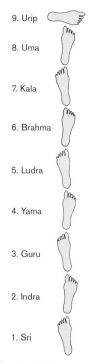

9. Urip

8. Uma

7. Kala

6. Brahma

5. Ludra

4. Yama

3. Guru

2. Indra

1. Sri

Changing Values

Identical units of measurement change their value in terms of their symbolic significance, depending on how many are used in a particular situation. The unit *tampak hatis*, which is the length of the house owner's foot and is used to measure the distance between structures in the compound, has eight distinct significances, after which the cycle repeats itself. Rather like 'Tinker, tailor, soldier, sailor'—the children's game of counting cherry stones—the final unit in the overall measurement will determine the character of the dimension and hence the qualities of the building to which it relates, sealing the fate of its occupants, as it were. A little extra is always added to the overall dimension—in the case of *tampak hatis*, the width of the house owner's foot—which is said to bring 'life' (*urip*) to the building.

The Balinese Architectural Lexicon

Building a Balinese house is as much a ritual process as it is a practical undertaking. Correct alignment with the sacred mountain, Gunung Agung, is an important consideration but many other ritual prescriptions govern the orientation, building methods and dimensions of every kind of built structure in the Balinese architectural lexicon.

Asta Kosali

The rules relating to the ritual and practical aspects of Balinese architecture are codified in sacred texts deposited with the village priests. These ancient documents, inscribed by hand on lontar palm manuscripts, are called the *Asta Kosali* or *Asta Kosalia*. The title probably derives from the Sanskrit words, *hasta* (hand) and *kausalya* (skill).

The *Asta Kosali* is consulted and interpreted in relation to specific circumstances by the *undagi*, or local architect-builder, who is an expert in rituals relating to architecture. Every aspect of construction and design, including shape, size, directional orientation and position of buildings in relation to other structures, is exhaustively documented in this Balinese building manual, which even prescribes the type of social background from which the builders of a particular type of structure should be recruited.

These texts are usually written in what is known as Jawa Kuno or Kawi, a semi-sacred language used in prayers and invocations to the gods. Kawi is never used in daily life and, though related to Balinese, is virtually unintelligible to anyone who has

not received a formal education in it. Although these building regulations are available for inspection by anyone who wishes to consult them, the arcane nature of the language means that in practice only language experts and priests are likely to do so. Instead carpenters and builders generally learn their trade by a kind of informal apprenticeship and the sacred texts are usually referred to only when there is disagreement about procedures or when constructing rarely-erected types of building.

Building for the Future

The design and construction of a Balinese dwelling is literally seen as determining the fate of its future occupants and the *Asta Kosali* provides a detailed account of the unfortunate consequences that will result from disregarding the rules. Failure to adhere to the prescriptions of the *Asta Kosali* is always dangerous and typically involves the contraction of some awful disease, death by accident or murder, unfaithful spouses, poverty and the loss of the affection of the gods. These are indeed dire consequences and any mistakes in the process of construction must be carefully rectified in the prescribed manner in order to avert ill effects. Conversely, good fortune and prosperity will come to those who stick closely to the regulations. These benefits include the accumulation of wealth in the form of gold and silver, family health, a faithful wife, loving children, and loyal servants.

Most of the rules have to do with the size and proportion of individual buildings and their relationship to one another in terms of the distance between them and their positioning inside the residential compound.

These regulations extend to the internal dimensions of a building: room sizes, thickness of walls and so forth. Some measurements have both good and bad connotations requiring difficult choices on the part of the house builder. For example, the unit of measurement known as *patokan tujuh rasa* will encourage the accumulation of material wealth but is also likely to foster disobedient and ill-mannered children.

The Human Body as a Ruler

In many Indonesian societies, the human body provides a metaphorical model for representing divisions of space within the house. In the case of the Balinese residential compound, the family shrine is identified with the head; the sleeping quarters and pavilion for receiving guests with the arms; the central courtyard with the navel; the hearth, with the sexual organs; the kitchen and granary, with legs and feet; and the refuse pit in the backyard, with the anus.

This anthropocentric frame of reference extends to include units of measurement that are based on bodily dimensions derived from those of the house owner's own body. These standard measurements are used to determine both the size and position of a building within the residential compound and also to calculate the dimensions of individal structural elements. Each measurement has a specific name and symbolic significance attached to its use.

The basic unit of measurement is called *depa asta musti*, which is a combination of the distance between the tip of the middle finger of each hand when the arms are stretched out horizontally on either side of the body (*depa*), plus the distance from the elbow to the tip of the middle finger (*hasta*), plus the width of the fist with thumb extended (*musti*).

These dimensions are recorded on a length of bamboo, which serves as a kind of yardstick for laying out the compound and the buildings within it.

Other critical units of measurement include the span of an outstretched hand from the thumb to the tip of the little finger (*lengkat*) and the width of a closed hand with the thumb placed over the first finger (*a musti*). The Balinese also measure in feet, both lengthways (*tampak*) and by width (*tampak ngandang*).

Mantra

The *Asta Kosali* also prescribes the type of mantra, or incantation, that should be recited to accompany each and every stage of construction.

Particular attention is paid to the process of selecting the timber. These are the lengthiest mantras and involve descriptions of all the types of trees that may be employed for building, while invoking the blessings of the many gods and spirits associated with trees and forests, the earth and the sky.

There are also mantras to bless the plot of land prior to commencing building. These praise the major Hindu deities of the Balinese pantheon. Special attention is paid to the blessing of holy water used in the consecration of the site.

The recitation of mantras is usually accompanied by a litany of all the dangers and misfortunes associated with incorrectly carrying out the prescribed procedures.

It is emphasised that neither the rituals nor the construction itself can be effectively conducted by those whose thoughts are less than pure.

Applying Measurements

Having established standard units of measurement, the *Asta Kosali* then describes how they should be applied. For example, the dimensions of house posts are based on those of the hand. The ideal width for an upright is equivalent to five knuckles, identified as the sign of the 'five Brahmans' (Hindu priests) and considered to have religious significance. Height is based on a composite measurement derived from the length of the index finger (*rahi*) and the gap between the second and third joints of the same digit (*guli madu*; the exact measurement is decided according to skin wrinkles and the width of the little finger (*anyari kacing*). These measurements are recorded on a bamboo stick.

Musti

Hasta

Depa

7

Architecture and Social Status

Balinese domestic architecture is closely linked to notions of rank and social status, with different rules and building regulations prescribed for different classes of person depending on their standing in the social hierarchy. Caste plays a central role, being the ultimate determinant of an individual's social status, irrespective of wealth or personal achievement.

Caste and Social Status

Bali's caste system has its origins in ancient India but time and local circumstances have endowed it with a uniquely Balinese character. There are four basic divisions of society: three noble castes, collectively named *triwangsa*, and beneath them the commoners (*sudra*). The *triwangsa* are subdivided into the princely caste of royalty and warriors (*satriya*), priests (*brahmana*) and merchants (*wesia*). Rank is signalled by the use of titles and there are subtle distinctions of status within each caste, based on genealogical descent. For instance, Balinese royalty and other members of the princely *satriya* caste like to trace their family origins

back to the 14th century when Javanese colonisers first established themselves as the ruling elite in Bali following the Majapahit conquest of the island. Prominent *brahmana* families, on the other hand, claim their descent from the famous Javanese priest Danghyang Nirartha, who was responsible for a Hindu revival in Bali in the mid-16th century. Social interactions between the castes are fixed by conventions of speech and habit. There are three main linguistic forms: high (*alus*), middle (*madia*) and low (*kasar*) Balinese, used according to the relative status of the interlocutors.

A Matter of Proportion

The dimensions of a residential compound are carefully determined according to the owner's caste. Size matters less than proportion. For example, only a raja may erect a square or nearly square compound where the difference in length between two sides is less than one unit of measurement. The merchant caste may build nearly square compounds, so long as the difference in the length of the sides is more than two, but less than four, units. Village headmen, on the other hand, should allow for a difference of three units between the two sides. Regulations like these cover each and every social category or caste affiliation.

The main units of measurement are *depa* (the distance from fingertip to fingertip when one's arms are held out horizontally on either side of the body), *hasta* (the length of the hand measure from the elbow to the tip of the index finger), and *a musti* (the width of the closed hand with thumb

Gateways
In terms of the degree of ornamentation and elaboration, there is little to distinguish the entrance to the compound of a commoner from that of a nobleman, although in the case of royal palaces the main gateways to the palace precincts are remarkable for their rich sculptures and ornate profile, which in many respects echo the entrances to temples. The example illustrated here is from the royal palace at Amlapura, formerly known as Karangasem.

Pavilion in Ubud Royal Palace.

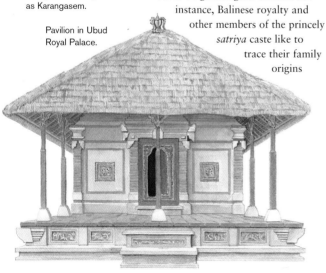

placed on top). Differences in rank and social status are reflected in different combinations of these basic units of measurement. There are three main categories: grand (*agung*) or best (*utama*); intermediate (*tengah*); and low (*rendah*). Measurements involving the third, or 'sweet', finger (*jari manis*), for example, typically belong to the *agung* scheme of things. *Agung* and *utama* dimensions are much the same in terms of the actual measurements employed, but are distinguished by social evaluation: *utama* specifications are used for the houses of the wealthy, whereas only members of the aristocracy are entitled to use *agung* dimensions. Significantly, the *Asta Kosali* only prescribes the minimum dimensions of a structure, which means that the compound of a commoner may actually be larger, if he can afford it, than that of an aristocrat.

From Pekarangan to Puri

The humblest type of compound, in terms of status, is that of the common man (*sudra*). This compound is called a *pekarangan* ('enclosure'). Its basic structures include a place for sleeping (*meten*); various pavilions (*bale*) for daily activities and for receiving guests; a cookhouse (*paon*); and a rice granary (*lumbung*). These are arranged around a clear central area (*natar*). The most auspicious (*kaja-kangin*) corner of the enclosure is reserved for the household temple (*sanggah*) which contains the shrines dedicated to ancestors.

The residential compounds of the three high castes are built using the same principles as the common man's but their proportions and degree of elaboration will differ. The simplest type is the *jero*, which is very similar to the *pekarangan*. The main difference is that members of the *triwangsa* castes are allowed to erect a *bale gede*—a rather grand,

open-sided pavilion whose roof is supported by twelve posts—whereas commoners may not. The *bale gede* has many uses: women weave there, artisans practise their craft, children play there when it rains, and people sleep in it at night. The *bale gede* also has an important role in family rites of passage.

Another type of pavilion, called a *bale dwaja* ('flag pavilion'), is reserved for members of the princely *satriya* caste, while the delightfully named *bale lembu-gajah* pavilion (literally, 'cow-elephant pavilion') is deemed especially suitable for the home of a Hindu or Buddhist priest.

Priests and Princes

Jero and *pekarangan* consist of single courtyards or dwelling compounds but a Brahman who becomes a priest (*pedanda*)—and not everyone of the *brahmana* caste becomes a priest—is entitled to a more elaborate residence (*grya*) with internal courtyards or divisions. The palace precincts (*puri*) of a royal family will be similarly subdivided into courtyards, each with specific uses relating to royal duties or prerogatives. Nevertheless, the same basic architectural principles still apply as far as orientation and the hierarchical organisation of space according to the Balinese compass rose are concerned, so that one can discern a common conceptual unity linking the humblest *pekarangan* with the grandest palace.

Bale Gede

Only members of the three aristocratic castes (*triwangsa*) are entitled to build themselves a *bale gede*. It is an almost square building located on the eastern side of the compound, just below the enclosure for the family shrines. Twelve posts support the roof and there may be a couple of wooden platforms at the back for sitting or sleeping. Typically it is an open-sided structure with only a partial wall or wooden screens at the back of the wooden platforms. Significantly, it is the only building in the compound, other than the family shrines, to have a pointed roof, all the other roofs being hipped. A pointed roof is associated with the idea of sacredness. The *bale gede* may be used for a number of activities: it is a place where women weavers set up their looms, where artisans practise their craft, where children play when it rains, and where people sleep at night. It also plays an important role in family rites of passage. These include the celebrations held 40 days after the birth of a child, tooth-filing ceremonies, and marriage rites. The *bale gede* is also the place where the corpse is laid out following a death in the family.

Building Materials and Construction Techniques

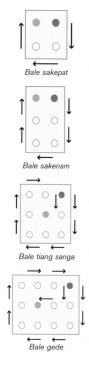

Pegged mortis and tenon joint.

Movement to the Right

Movement to the Right

The first post to be erected should be the one that stands at the *kaja-kangin* corner of the building, the most auspicious position in terms of the Balinese compass rose. An offering platform is attached near the top of this post and the erection of the rest of the posts is determined by the law of 'movement to the right', an idea found all over Indonesia. In the case of Bali this means more specifically in a clockwise direction.

Bale sakepat

Bale sakenam

Bale tiang sanga

Bale gede

The structure of Balinese buildings can be considered in terms of the local *tri angga* classification system, which assumes that everything in the natural world can be divided into the three components of *nista, madya* and *utama* (see page four).

These categories are hierarchically ordered in terms of a set of spatial coordinates—high, middle and low—that in the case of Balinese buildings are identified with the stereobate or base *(nista)*, timber house posts and curtain walls *(madya)*, and the roof *(utama)*.

Stereobate

The base typically consists of four low walls of brick or stone, in-filled with stamped earth. In unimportant or humble buildings, this packed earth surface will also be the floor, but where finances allow, it will be paved. Similarly the walls of the base may be plain, profiled or carved with reliefs depending on the nature of the building and the status and wealth of the owner.

Timber Frame

The main load-bearing elements of the building consist of a timber post-and-beam framework. This structure supports the hipped roof, which is formed from a coconut wood and bamboo frame covered with grass thatch *(alang alang)* or, in the case of more affluent households, clay tiles.

The height of the posts *(adegan)* is determined by measurements taken from the house owner's body, and the dimensions of the house posts in turn determine the proportions of the building. The standard unit of measurement for house posts is a

rahi, the length of a line drawn between the end of the lifeline at the base of the thumb, and the tip of the index finger. Optimal heights are 20, 21 or 22 *rahi*.

A measurement of 19 *rahi* is expressly avoided, the explanation being that it would expose the occupants of the house to disease, crime and other misfortunes. The latter measurement is sometimes referred to as *buta dengan milara* and it is said to be the cause of unhappy love affairs.

The posts rest on masonry or stone column bases called *umpak*, and the rigidity of the structure is established by tie-beams which are stiffened at the joints by shores or brackets. Individual components are joined by mortise and tenon, or lap joints, and are secured by a wedge or wooden peg.

The *Asta Kosali* prescribes what kinds of timber should be used for particular building requirements. Traditionally, the preferred material for house posts is teak, which ideally should be cut from a living tree growing locally, although teak imported from Kalimantan or Java is considered to be superior.

Offerings must be made before the tree is felled and, when the posts are ready to be raised into position, care must be taken to ensure that they are erected according to the direction of growth of the tree trunk from which they were cut, with the root end being placed in the foundations and the growing tip end supporting the roof. On no account may posts be erected 'upside down', that is to say, with the direction of growth inverted.

Walls

The walls of Balinese houses are made from stone, brick or even simply mud. They do not carry any load, being completely detached from the timber structure that supports the roof.

The favoured building material is *paras*, a kind of soft sandstone that is cut into uniform brick-sized blocks and then gently baked in the sun.

Using muddy water for mortar, these bricks are rubbed back and forth on the preceding course until they stick. When the mud is still wet, it provides an element of adhesion, but subsequently the wall is held together simply by its weight and the near-perfect fit between courses. *Paras* is a very plastic material, which can be easily carved, but is not very durable and soon deteriorates when exposed to the elements, hence the ancient appearance of many Balinese buildings, despite the fact that most structures are no more than a few years old.

The Balinese also employ adobe as a building material. This is made locally from wet earth kneaded into balls and placed in the sun to dry.

Walls are constructed by placing these mud balls in parallel rows and then filling the crevices with more mud. Another layer is added on top and the process repeated until the desired elevation is achieved.

Adobe is even less durable than *paras* and always has a protective coping of thatch that is usually made from rice straw. Rice-straw thatch does not itself last very long and is usually renewed after each harvest.

Roofs

Since the materials used to make walls are not very durable, care is taken to ensure that the walls are well protected from the elements by widely overhanging eaves. The main framework is made of bamboo with the roof ridge supported by king posts, girders and columns.

The usual roofing material used in ordinary buildings is a thick thatch that is made from *alang alang* grass (*Imperata sp.*). The grass is gathered in bundles which are doubled over the midrib of coconut fronds and stitched in place. These sections of thatching

Alang alang thatch.

are lashed onto the bamboo framework of the roof using red-dyed rattan cords or ties made from the natural fibre of the sugar palm (*Arenga pinnata*), with extra thatch along the ridges.

Lastly, the roof is combed with a special type of rake and the bottom edge is trimmed with a knife. Such a roof, which may be up to 50 centimetres in thickness, can last for many years.

More important structures may employ locally made clay pantiles, or even modern Marseilles tiles, while split bamboo shingles are a popular choice for roofing material in mountain regions.

In the case of religious structures and family shrines, black thatch (*ijuk*) from the sugar palm is used instead of *alang alang*.

House post

- *Sulur*
- *Adegan/ tiang* ('Post')
- *Jongkok asu* ('Squatting dog')
- *Umpak*
- *Sendi* ('Base')

11

Grid layout of the compound

Conceptually, the Balinese residential compound can be divided in accordance with the *nawa-sanga* scheme of things into nine squares consisting of the eight cardinal directions and the centre. The family shrines are positioned in the most auspicious corner of the compound: 'towards the mountains' (*kaja*) and 'to the east' (*kangin*). The sleeping pavilion (*meten*) of the householder, which is the next most important building in the compound, is positioned immediately to the west of the family temple, which reflects not only the senior position of the family head but also his relative proximity to the ancestors in terms of descent.

Kaja Kauh	Kaja	Kaja Kangin
Kauh	Puseh	Kangin
Kelod Kauh	Kelod	Kelod Kangin

Layout of the Compound

As we have seen, measurement and orientation play a crucial role in Balinese architecture, and one of the most important stages in construction is at the very beginning when the overall dimensions of the compound are marked out and the ground plan of the different structures, and their relative position and proximity to one another, are laid out on the ground.

This is a critical time that will determine both the character of the buildings erected and the potential fate of those who will occupy them.

Measuring the Sides

The first set of dimensions that must be determined, once the site of the compound has been selected, is its length and width overall. The basic unit of measurement employed here is the distance between the fingertips of the two hands when the arms are fully outstretched on either side of the body (*depa*). The sum of the lengths of two sides must add up to an odd number of these units, and their difference in length, when one is subtracted from the other, should also be an odd number of units. If there is a mistake in the measurements and their sum or difference happens to be an even number of units, it is said that the compound is 'without doors', 'closed', or 'blocked'. It is also said to be 'like a body without a soul', in other words 'dead' (*mati*). The explanation given is that a compound without doors provides no access for the gods and at the same time prevents the expulsion of malevolent influences. Such a site cannot support life, hence its designation as moribund.

Site Rituals

The various stages of construction and the eventual occupancy date are determined by auspicious dates in the Balinese calendar. Construction is inaugurated by the rite of *suci daksina peras ajuman panyeneng*, which is intended to purify the site. This rite involves placing supplicatory offerings at the 'mountain' (*kaja*) end of the compound. A similar offering is also placed at the *kelod* end to placate malevolent spirits and other harmful agencies (*buta kala*). Each subsequent stage of construction must be accompanied by further offerings to negate malign influences.

Layout of the Compound

The first thing to be constructed after the inaugural rites are the compound walls. Once these are completed, temporary shrines are erected in the place where the family temple will eventually be built.

Work then starts on laying out the rest of the compound in accordance with the spatial precepts of the Balinese compass rose. The latter can be seen in terms of a grid consisting of a rectangle, corresponding to the perimeter wall of the compound, subdivided into nine 'squares'. Each square represents one of the eight cardinal and inter-cardinal points of

Deities and Dimensions

Units of Measurement	Deity	Status or Attribute	Compass Direction
One	(Dewi) Sri	Goddess of Rice	*Kaja-kangin*
Two	Indra	Lord of the Heavens	*Kangin*
Three	Guru	Supreme Teacher	*Kelod-kangin*
Four	Yama	Lord of Hell	*Kelod*
Five	Rudra	Dissolver of Life	*Kelod-kauh*
Six	Brahma	God of Fire	*Kauh*
Seven	Kala	Lord of Darkness	*Kaja-kauh*
Eight	Uma	Mother of all Nature	*Kaja*

the compass, while the ninth square occupies the centre.

Distance and Position

The first building to be erected in the compound is the householder's sleeping pavilion (*meten*). All subsequent structures are laid out in relation to this starting-out point. The distance between buildings and their position in relation to the compound's walls is critical.

The principal unit of measurement employed is the length of the house owner's foot (*tampak*), and again the number of units for a particular dimension is calculated by reference to the Balinese compass rose.

The system works as follows: each of the four cardinal points, and their intermediaries, are associated with a particular deity in the Balinese Hindu pantheon and as the compound is measured out in paces, the names of the deities are recited (see page six). A single pace is identified with the rice goddess Sri, two paces with Indra, three paces with Guru, and so on until one arrives at eight paces (Uma), whereupon the cycle begins again.

Each deity is also associated with one of the cardinal directions and a particular set of attributes (see table) that together determine the number of units employed in setting out the dimensions of individual buildings. The householder's sleeping pavilion, for example, is the most important structure in the compound after the family temple, and for this reason should be located at the *kaja* end. In southern Bali, where most of the island's population live, *kaja* roughly corresponds to north, this being the direction of the central mountain range. Consequently, the sleeping pavilion should be placed eight *tampak*, or multiples thereof, from the *kaja*-most wall, because the number eight is associated with the deity Uma, who in this scheme of things is identified with the north.

The cookhouse, on the other hand, should be set out at a distance of six *tampak*, or multiples thereof, to the south of the owner's pavilion since the number six is identified with Brahma, who is in turn associated with fire and, in this context, with the hearth.

Similar considerations apply for other structures in the compound whose relative positions must be carefully worked out in order to ensure that all is for the best in the best of all possible worlds.

Position of the Entrance

The main entrance to the Balinese compound should ideally be placed on the west (*kauh*) side and at the seaward (*kelod*) end. For various reasons this is not always possible, in which case the 'blind' wall (*aling aling*) that stands just behind the doorway is designed so that anyone coming into the compound must first proceed towards the *kelod-kauh* end before they reach the centre of the compound around which the main buildings are arranged.

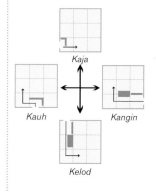

Kaja

Kauh

Kangin

Kelod

Kaja

Key
1. Temporary family shrine.
2. *Meten* (sleeping pavilion).
3. *Paon* (cookhouse).
4. Entrance and *aling aling* wall.

The Dwelling Compound

Paduraksa
The salients at the four corners of the compound are intended to impede bad feelings arising within the compound from being broadcast abroad and conversely to prevent malign influences from entering from outside. These bastions against the passage of malevolency in and out of the compound are called *paduraksa*. *Padu* means 'corner' and *raksa* means 'guardian'.

Entrances
Balinese compounds have only one entrance, on the side bordering the street. Entrances define the threshold between inside and out and are viewed ambivalently—although they may admit welcome visitors they may also allow in malign influences. Thus the entrance belongs to the vile sphere and should therefore be located at the compound's *kelod* end, and to the west. Moreover, a small wall (*aling-aling*) is placed directly behind the doorway. This screens off the interior, but more importantly it obstructs the entry of malevolent spirits, which are believed to have difficulty making abrupt changes of direction.

The Balinese residential compound is home to an extended family typically consisting of a married couple, their married sons with their wives and children, their unmarried daughters, and, if still alive, the parents of the husband. In the case of low-caste families, however, the property usually passes to the last-born son and non-inheriting sons will either build their own house compound or move in with their wives. If a group of brothers decides to stay together, each brother will have his own living quarters within the compound with its own kitchen facilities.

A Hierarchy of Levels
The level inside the compound is generally a little higher than that of the street outside. This serves both a practical and a symbolic function. On the one hand it makes it easier to provide drainage for the compound simply by creating conduits that empty into a ditch running on either side of the road. On the other hand the superior elevation is part of a hierarchical ordering of space that runs from the street to the family temple situated in the *kaja-kangin* corner of the compound. The latter is the highest point in the compound, reflecting its status as sacred ground.

The Family Temple
The family temple (*sanggah*) is set off from the rest of the compound by a low wall and provides a sacred enclosure (*pamerajan*) for the family shrines. The relative dimensions of this walled-off space are governed by ritual prescriptions similar to those that regulate the shape and size of the compound as a whole. Different dimensions have different significances. For example, the gods are

said to favour a family whose *sanggah* enclosure is only one unit longer than it is wide; even higher esteem is attached to those whose place of worship differs by two units, and great purity where the difference is one of five units. These attributions are not always positive: marriage to an unfaithful wife may be the fate of those where the difference between length and width is eight units.

The location of the entrance to the *sanggah* enclosure is also important and should ideally be placed between the sleeping pavilion (*umah meten*) of the family head and the *bale kangin*, the pavilion occupying the eastern side of the central court. A north-facing entrance is considered to be particularly inauspicious.

Gods and Ancestors
The family temple contains a number of different shrines, dedicated to both the gods and family ancestors. The most prominent is the *sanggah kamulan*, a small, wooden, house-like construction raised on pillars and standing on a sandstone or brick column. This structure is divided into three compartments, dedicated to the Hindu triumvirate (*trimurti*) of Brahma, Siwa and Vishnu. Brahma is

associated with male ancestors of the household, while Vishnu is identified with the female. Ideally, a Balinese man should build one of these shrines when he marries.

The *sanggah kamulan* stands in the *kaja-kangin* corner of the temple enclosure, together with other ritual structures dedicated to Mother Earth (Ibu Pretiwi) and the sacred mountains, Mt Agung and Mt Batur. The rice goddess, Sri, shares a shrine (panegtegan) with the deities of wealth and knowledge, Rambut Sedana and Saraswati, respectively. There may also be an altar dedicated to the sun god, Surya.

Other ritual structures can also be located in the *kaja-kangin* corner of the temple enclosure, dedicated to one or more of several different gods and goddesses. These structures vary according to the status of the head of the family. There will also be a number of brick and sandstone columns around the compound where offerings can be placed for the spirits who guard the home and its occupants.

Sleeping, Eating and Bathing

The Balinese compound appears to lack what Western visitors would recognise as adequate provision for sleeping, eating and bathing. The head of the family sleeps in the most prestigious pavilion in the compound, the *umah meten*, which he inherits from his parents when they die. This is situated along the *kaja* wall of the central courtyard, which not only reflects the status of the family head but also identifies his position as closest to the ancestors.

Children and their mothers tend to sleep in the *bale sakepat* but other family members sleep wherever they choose—typically in one of the open-sided pavilions around the central courtyard (natar) or the platform beneath the rice granary.

There are seldom any bathing facilities within the compound, though piped water has altered the situation in recent years, and people take their bath in rivers, water conduits and specially constructed village bathing pools.

A typical shrine from a family temple.

Key

1. Entrance.
2. *Aling-aling*.
'Blind' wall.
3. *Natar* or *latar*.
A level, open yard in the centre of the compound, which is kept free of built structures.
4. *Sanggah*.
Family temple.
5. *Umah meten*.
Sleeping pavilion for the head of the family.
6. *Bale tiang sanga*.
Pavilion for receiving guests.
7. *Bale sakepat*.
Pavilion where children and other junior members of the family sleep.
8. *Bale sakenam*.
Traditionally a place where women do their weaving.
9 and 10. The kitchen (paon) and rice barn (lumbung) occupy the 'lowest' part of the site, at the seaward (kelod) end of the compound, which in the nawa-sanga system is the domain of Vishnu, the preserver and governor. Significantly, Vishnu is identified with female ancestors, the kitchen and granary being primarily regarded as the domain of women.

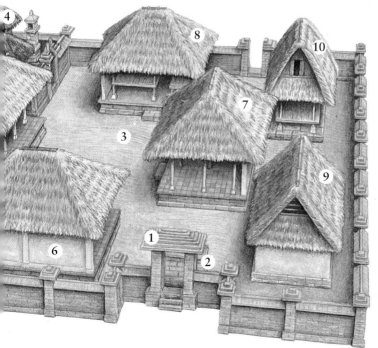

Ground Plan

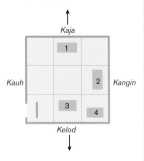

Kaja ↑

Kauh | Kangin

Kelod ↓

1. *Meten*–sleeping pavilion.
2. *Bale sakenam.*
3. *Paon*–cookhouse.
4. *Lumbung*–granary.

Pavilions

The typical Balinese residential compound consists of a number of different structures grouped around a central courtyard.

Each building is associated with a particular function or activity and has a specific location in the family compound.

The Balinese people classify these structures according to the number of posts used in their construction. A building that employs four posts to support the roof is therefore called a *bale sakepat* (*bale* = pavilion, *sakasa* = post, *empat* = four), a *bale sakenam* is a six-post structure (*enam* = six), and so on up to the maximum of twelve posts.

Most of these buildings are raised on a masonry stereobate, or plinth, and are open on one or more sides. The roof is supported by a timber and bamboo frame; walls, where they exist, are not designed to carry any load, but simply constitute a screen to give some protection from the elements and provide a degree of privacy.

Umah meten

The first building to be erected, after the construction of temporary shrines in the *kaja-kangin* corner of the compound, is the sleeping pavilion (*umah meten*) of the house owner. This is located to the west of the family temple, but still at the *kaja* end of the compound. It is a rectangular structure with four solid, windowless walls, and a single entrance positioned in the middle of the elevation facing the centre of the compound. The interior consists simply of a pair of wooden sleeping platforms (*pedeman*) positioned on either side of the door.

The *umah meten* of the common man is an eight-pillar structure, but, in the case of higher-caste families, the stereobate is extended to create a verandah or porch in front of the entrance with another line of posts supporting the roof.

The *umah meten* is where the family sleeps and keeps its valuables —gold, silver, jewellery and the family kris (ceremonial dagger). It is also traditionally the place for

12-column meten
Commoners are not permitted to build their *umah meten* with a verandah. Significantly, the *umah meten* in a priest's compound may have a pyramidal hipped roof, like those used for shrines and other religious structures.

giving birth—the term *meten* is derived from the word *metu* meaning 'to come out' or 'to be born'.

The building may also be used during periods of ritual restriction, which are required before certain rites of passage that mark significant events in a person's life, such as tooth-filing or the first menstruation. In this respect the *meten* is perceived in ritual terms as the family womb, a place where children are born and where changes of status, seen here as a kind of symbolic rebirth, occur.

Although normally occupied by the head of the family and his wife, the *umah meten* may be vacated for newly-weds or unmarried girls, for it is the only place in the compound where privacy is available.

Paon

The kitchen is usually a fairly simple structure, built on a low plinth and often employing a gable roof which is easier to construct than the hipped alternative. Earthen charcoal- or wood-burning stoves are built along the rear wall and pots and pans are slung overhead. Traditionally, there would also be large earthenware water-storage jars, though a piped water supply is more common in most areas today.

Lumbung

The granary is a more elaborate affair than other buildings in the compound. Its floor is raised high off the ground on posts that stand on foundation stones rather than a stereobate or masonry plinth like other structures. Sometimes there is an intermediate platform raised a little off the ground, but below the floor of the granary. This provides a cool, shady

workplace by day and somewhere to sleep at night. *Lumbung* designs vary from one part of the island to another, but the distinctive hull-shaped roof with horseshoe gable ends can generally be seen in the southern areas. Often one sees wooden discs on top of the foundation posts. These are intended to deter rodents from climbing up and nibbling away at the rice harvest.

Rice farming is a very special activity in Balinese eyes, rice itself being perceived as a gift of the gods. Not surprisingly, the filling of the granary with a newly harvested crop is an important moment in each agricultural season and it is traditionally accompanied by rituals dedicated to Dewi Sri, who is the goddess of agriculture and fertility. In the past, the newly harvested rice was taken from the fields while still in its panicle and stored directly in the *lumbung*. Nowadays, however, the modern, fast-growing strains of rice are threshed and winnowed in the fields and it is the hulled rice that is taken back to the granary.

Lumbung.

Paon.

Bale sakenam

The Balinese pavilion is a fairly utilitarian structure and may be used for a number of purposes. 'Fitted' platforms for sleeping and other activities are a regular feature.

Decorative Features

Carved beam.

Although the Balinese people are renowned for their artistic and creative energies, Balinese domestic architecture is not subject to a great degree of decorative elaboration or ornamentation, except in the case of royal palaces and the homes of wealthy members of the *triwangsa* castes. Decoration of ordinary houses, where it does occur, is typically reserved for wooden components.

The shafts of house posts may be given a distinctive sculpted profile, while the brackets supporting beams may be enlivened by ornate foliate embellishment.

Doors are typically panelled and carved wooden friezes or ventilation grilles are also commonplace. These decorative elements are painted, but in the case of royal palaces and other important structures, such as the *bale gede* pavilion in the compound of a high caste family, such ornamented surfaces may also be gilded with gold leaf.

Masonry walls stand on a stepped foundation, and are topped by a decorative cornice or coping, while the surfaces of the base of pavilions are sometimes ornamented with reliefs. In Majapahit times, in temples and palaces, it was also common to insert ceramics into the brickwork—for example, Ming porcelain or Vietnamese exportware.

Capital and column from a rice barn.

Like other Balinese structures, the dimensions of an entrance are endowed with symbolic or ritual significance linked to the unit of measurement used in setting it out, the type of ritual employed in its consecration, and the particular deity—for example, Mahadewi, Saraswati or Sri—to whom it is dedicated. There are places for offerings on either side of the entrance. These may either be a pair of niches in the external wall or two free-standing offering columns (*apit lawang*) on either side of the doorway.

The positioning of decorative features on buildings is likely to be significant: birds, for example, will adorn the upper parts of a structure, being creatures of the air, while representations of malevolent beings are nearer ground level, reflecting their associations with the infernal nether regions of the Balinese Hades.

In the case of *triwangsa* residences, the family temple in the *kaja-kangin* corner of the compound is surrounded by a perforated wall known as an *ancak saji* wall: a honeycomb effect is created by leaving spaces between the building blocks, after which the wall receives a Gaudi-like treatment with the insertion of glazed tiles and other ceramic pieces.

One of the most striking images in Balinese iconography is the face of a leering monster, with lolling tongue, bulging eyes and ferociously large canines. It is typically found over the monumental gateway (*kori agung*) of palaces and temples. This is the face of the Bhoma, whose fearful countenance is intended to drive away malevolent influences.

In royal palaces, much effort and expense goes into the construction of monumental gateways. These resemble temple portals and perform much the same role—to demarcate the realm of ordinary life from some other plane of existence, the one sacred, the other political, though in the traditional scheme of things, the personage of the ruler was as much endowed with a mystical efficacy as

with temporal power, for the two were part and parcel of the same phenomenon.

In temples, the most important and most elaborate carvings are reserved for the walls and gates, for these form the division between the sacred ground of the temple and the profane ground outside it. Temple reliefs often depict well-known scenes or episodes from Indian Classical literature. The *Ramayana* and *Mahabharata* epics provide a rich source of inspiration; other favourites include erotic encounters from the *Arjuna Wiwaha* which portray luscious nymphs making passionate love to the god Arjuna, and charming vignettes from the *tantri* tales, the Balinese equivalent of Aesop's fables from Classical Greek literature.

Often there can be a humorous element to these representations; the Mexican painter Miguel Covarrubias, who lived in Bali in the early 1930s, likened the reliefs in north Bali to American-style comic strips. A well-known example at the Pura Dalem, Jagaraga, near Singaraja, shows a car driven by bearded foreigners being held up by a gangster armed with a revolver, while at the nearby Pura Meduwe Karang, in Kubutambahan, there is an image of a European man riding a bicycle with a lotus flower for a rear wheel. The latter is said to portray the Dutch artist W.O.J. Nieuwenkamp, who visited Bali in the early years of the 20th century.

Doorway frieze
Doors in Bali, which often incorporate ventilation grilles, are usually panelled and generally surmounted by a decorative frieze. The example here features the leering face of Bhoma, grinning at us rather like the Cheshire cat in Tenniel's illustration for *Alice in Wonderland*.

Bhoma head
This Bhoma head is from Desa Pakudi, Gianyar. The image is clearly related to the *kala* heads found over the doorways of Javanese temples dating from Indonesia's Classical, Hindu-Buddhist era.

Painted wooden decoration from a family temple, Sebatu.

The Balinese Village

Village assemblies (*sangkepan desa*), attended by family heads, are held every month, at the *pura puseh* or at the assembly hall (*bale agung*) nearby, during which matters of both ritual and secular importance are addressed.

One of the principal responsibilities of the village assembly is to organise the anniversary celebrations (*odalan*) of each of the village temples. These 'birthday' festivals, which fall every 210 days according to the Balinese ceremonial *wuku* calendar, are extremely important to the life of the community, being intended to ritually cleanse the village territory (*tanah desa*) and purify all the members of the temple congregation. Everyone in the local community is drawn into the preparation of offerings and organising the various entertainments. These include gamelan recitals, shadow puppet theatre (*wayang kulit*), human dance-dramas (*wayang wong* and *gambuh*), masked dances (*topeng*) and operetta (*arja*), and are performed for the enjoyment of the gods and mortals alike.

The Balinese village is described by the word *desa*. This denotes both the settlement and its immediate physical environs (*tanah desa*) and at the same time refers to a religious community made up of local householders and their families who are responsible for maintaining the ritual purity and spiritual well-being of the *tanah desa*.

The latter is achieved by observing the local customary laws (*desa adat*) and by participation in the cycle of religious ceremonies that take place at the village temples.

Village Layout

The Balinese village is laid out on a *kaja-kelod* axis running between the mountains and the sea, often in defiance of local topographical considerations.

The approach is signalled by a *candi bentar* (split gateway), with the road typically executing a sharp S-bend a little after this. Like the *aling-aling* 'blind' wall immediately inside the entrance to the compound, the S-bend strategy outside it is another tactic intended to prevent malevolent spirits from entering the village—the spirits are said to

have difficulty negotiating sharp corners.

The centre of the community is typically defined by a crossroads and a large square, or *bancingah*,

Key
1. *Pura puseh* (ancestral temple).
2. *Pura desa* (main temple).
3. *Bancingah* (village square).
4. *Wantilan* (Cockfighting pavilion).
5. *Pura dalem* (temple for the dead) and graveyard.

hall (*bale agung*) and a drum tower (*bale kulkul*), for summoning the community to meetings. There may also be a special pavilion for holding cockfights. This is called a *wantilan* and is often quite an impressive structure with a soaring roof and elegant columns.

Kahyangan Tiga

Balinese villages should ideally have at least three temples, which between them serve the religious needs of the community.

In addition to the main village temple, which is situated at the centre of the village, there is also a temple honouring the founding fathers of the community and another dedicated to the dead. Their respective locations, in relation to the centre of the village, can be understood in the context of Balinese ideas of ritual sanctity and pollution: the ancestral temple (*pura puseh*) is placed at the *kaja* end of the village as befits the deified status of the community founders, while the temple for the dead, the *pura dalem*, is located at the *kelod* end, reflecting the polluting nature of death. By the same reasoning, the community graveyard and cremation ground too are, typically, situated nearby.

The practice of having three village temples is said to have been begun by Mpu Kuturan, the revered Javanese priest, sage and temple architect who was responsible for a reformation of Balinese Hinduism during the 11th century, at a time when the religion was in decline. The three temples are known collectively as the *kahyangan tiga* and they are identified with the Hindu trinity of Brahma, Vishnu and Siwa.

which is kept free of built structures but often has a huge banyan tree at one end to provide shade. The main village temple (*pura desa*) is usually located in the most propitious corner (*kaja-kangin*) of this open space, although the site may alternatively be occupied by the palace (*puri*) of a local prince.

Other important public buildings associated with the centre of the village include the local assembly

The Neighbourhood

Any village or settlement of reasonable size will consist of a number of smaller residential groupings or neighbourhoods, called *banjar*, each with their own local temple or *pura pamaskan*. Family compounds, belonging to the same *banjar*, tend to be laid out in rows on either side of a street or lane, and these rows of adjacent compounds, which are called *tempek*, often act together in performing the various communal duties or obligations. Each *banjar* has specific ritual duties to fulfil, not only in relation to its own neighbourhood temple, but also to the main village temples. *Banjar* members also act together in secular matters such as the maintenance of roads and the policing of the neighbourhood.

Public Buildings

Every Balinese village has a number of public buildings or spaces which serve various community needs.

They include the three principal village temples that make up the *kahyangan tiga* temple system, an assembly hall (*bale agung*), the village square and market place, and a cockfighting pavilion (*wantilan*).

These are the main focal points of the community, where village people come together at festivals and on other important social occasions to honour the gods, discuss village affairs, or just to meet and socialise with one another.

Village Guardians
The centre of a Balinese village is often presided over by a *rakshasa* statue, the village guardian. This one is in Batuan, Gianyar.

Candi Bentar

The threshold of the Balinese village is usually marked by a *candi bentar*, a split gateway. The *candi bentar*, which is a distinctive feature of Balinese architecture, is also used for temple entrances where it marks a transition from the secular world to the realm of the sacred.

In elevation the *candi bentar* has a characteristic stepped profile, lavishly decorated with carvings and reliefs. The two inner surfaces, as one passes through the gateway, are left sheer and unornamented.

The architectural origins of *candi bentar* can be traced to ancient Java and in particular to the East Javanese kingdom of Majapahit (late 13th– early 16th centuries), which was the last of the great Hindu-Buddhist empires in Indonesia's Classical past. Ruins in the vicinity of Trowulan, which archaeologists

A *bale kulkul* in the mountain village of Sutei.

Bale Kulkul

The *bale kulkul* is a tower-like structure and usually occupies a prominent position in the village. The *kulkul* itself is a percussive device consisting of a hollow piece of timber with a slit in one side. It resonates when struck, rather like a wooden tubular bell, and is beaten to summon the local community to assemble. Different rhythms indicate the specific reason for the summons—for example, a meeting of household heads at the *bale agung*, or, in the past, a call to arms. The building in which the *kulkul* is housed—it is usually suspended from the rafters of the roof—may be simple or elaborate, depending on the wealth of the community. The more extravagantly ornamented examples showcase the skill of the local stonemasons.

Bale kulkul (left) in Banjar Abiankapas, Denpasar.

have identified as the former capital of Majapahit, include a massive example of a *candi bentar*, which may have been the ceremonial entrance to the city.

The symbolic significance of this bifurcated gateway remains unclear, but the Mexican artist and writer Miguel Covarrubias, who lived in Bali during the 1930s, records a pleasing Balinese account. He writes that the *candi bentar* represents the legendary Mount Meru of Hindu mythology, which was split in two by Pasupati (Siwa) and placed in Bali as the twin peaks of Gunung Agung and Gunung Batur.

Wantilan

The cockfighting pavilion is a large and often quite imposing structure with a lofty tiled roof raised on twelve columns, and is typically found at the centre of the Balinese village. Cockfighting once played a central role in the social life of the

Balinese village, or at least in the lives of its menfolk, for women were prohibited from participating.

Today, it is strictly regulated by the Government, for all forms of gambling are illegal in the Republic of Indonesia, including betting on fighting cocks.

But cockfighting (*tajen*) has very deep and ancient roots in Balinese culture and because it involves the spilling of blood, it also has a ritual aspect to it, being seen as a propitiation to malevolent spirit influences (*bhuta* or *kala*).

Consequently the Indonesian Government does allow a limited number of cockfights to be held on ceremonial occasions provided no betting takes place.

Needless to say, this last stricture is never adhered to. Furthermore, cockfights are still regularly held almost everywhere on the island, albeit discreetly out of sight of the authorities.

Cockfighting Pavilion
One of the distinguishing features of the cockfighting pavilion (*wantilan*) is its pyramid-shaped roof, a characteristic it shares with shrines and other religious structures. The reason for this is that the *wantilan* is perceived as a sacred building—the shedding of blood during the cockfight is akin to offering a blood sacrifice to malevolent forces. This *wantilan* is at Banjar Tangkas, Kendran, in south Bali.

The main entrance to the palace precincts should be located at the *kelod* end of the complex, on the west (*kauh*) side. The courtyard is typically enclosed by a tracery wall (*ancak saji*) which gives the space an open feel. It is where the ruler meets his subjects, and where royal entertainments are held. There are usually several open pavilions for guests and to house the gamelan, while an impressive *kori agung* gateway leading into the next courtyard provides a dramatic point of entry for performers in other court theatricals. The central courtyard at the *kelod* end of the complex is called the *samanggen* and serves as the fore-court to the raja's quarters (*pelataran rangki*) at the centre of the palace precincts. In the final courtyard at this end of the palace complex, where they can be entered discretely by the raja's staff via a screened door, are the servant's quarters, kitchen and granary.

Balinese Palaces

In traditional Hindu cosmology, the territory of the kingdom was conceived, in symbolic terms, as replicating the universe as a whole, a microcosm of the macrocosm. In this respect, the seat of the ruler, which ideally was situated at or near the geographical centre of the kingdom, was seen not only as the ultimate source of temporal power but also as a cosmological and ritual centre. The two aspects of power went hand in hand, for the ruler in Classical Indonesia was regarded as divinely appointed.

Balinese Kingdoms

Following the conquest of Bali by the East Javanese Majapahit kingdom in the early 14th century, a vassal king was installed at Samprangan, near present-day Gianyar, who owed his allegiance to Java. The island was effectively a dependency of Java until the start of the 15th century, but, as Majapahit fortunes waned, Bali gradually gained its autonomy from Java and, following the collapse of Majapahit in the early years of the 16th century, grew to be an imperial power in its own right under the leadership of King Waturenggong. By the end of the next century Bali had fragmented into several lesser kingdoms. These survive today as eight regencies (*kabupaten*), Bali's local government departments.

At the Centre

The palace (*puri*) of the local dynastic ruler (raja) and his family should be auspiciously sited, ideally within the *kaja-kangin* quadrant formed by the crossroads at the centre of town. In practice, local circumstances and history may determine otherwise. For example, there may be more than one palace complex. At Karangasem, an older palace was left by the founders of a new dynasty to senior relatives, while at Bangli a new complex was built for younger relatives; where two earlier palaces occupy the centre of Bangli, the principal one is situated in the town's *kaja-kauh* quadrant.

Palace Layout

The palace resembles the basic pattern established for the residential compound of the common man, for it is laid out according to the same rules of the Balinese compass rose. For palaces, however, the grid-like division of the area enclosed by the perimeter walls is given a physical reality, with walls and doorways dividing the palace precincts into a series of interconnected courtyards.

The Dynastic Temple

The *kaja-kangin* sector of the grid is occupied, predictably, by the family temple (*pamerajan*) of the ruler, which in this instance forms a kind of cosmic centre of the political territory. Unlike ordinary family temples, it is open to the public on ceremonial occasions and is approached from the *kauh* side of the palace complex via two intermediary courtyards (*jaba* and *jaba tengah*). The first of these should ideally be situated on the western side of the palace complex and is entered from outside the palace walls via a ceremonial, split gateway (*candi bentar*). The second courtyard is used for the preparation of offerings and the reception of guests attending palace ceremonies. This courtyard is completely enclosed on all sides and is entered from the outer courtyard by another ceremonial gateway called a *kori agung*, which has a lintel and doors that can be shut. The *kori agung* is usually quite an ornate structure, with statuary and carvings intended to deter malevolent influences from entering the inner sanctum of the royal temple. The *aling-aling* wall inside the gateway is also decorated with reliefs, which often allude to the date of construction. The doorway in the *kori agung* is opened only on ceremonial occasions, with everyday access afforded by a smaller, less elaborate door to one side.

The sanctum sanctorum of the royal family temple (*jero-dalem*) contains the ancestral shrines of the ruling dynasty, which are much the same as other family shrines except that they are usually more numerous and more elaborately ornamented.

There will also be *meru* towers dedicated to the gods. The number of tiered roofs (*tumpang*) is always uneven; the exact count depends on the nature of the deity to whom the structure is dedicated and the status of the person responsible for its erection. For example, a raja who dedicates a *meru* to Siwa is entitled to build the maximum number of *tumpang*—eleven.

Raja's Residential Quarters
The most important of the three residential courts that occupy the central row of the palace complex is the middle one, which is where the raja and his family live. A wall bisects the court along an east-west axis and symbolises the division between the public and private lives of the ruler. The *kelod* half (*pelataran rangki*) is the public domain and is reached by members of the public from the *kelod* end of the palace complex. This court has a *bale gede* where important life-cycle rituals relating to members of the royal family take place and there is

also likely to be a pavilion to house important guests.

The *kaja* half of the central court is called the *saren agung* and this is occupied by the ruler and immediate family. The main building here is the living quarters (*ukiran*) of the raja himself. This should ideally be located exactly in the middle of the palace complex where it is divided in two by the wall that separates the central courtyard into its *kaja* and *kelod* halves. In this respect, the *ukiran* is located on the border of the public and private domains. The *ukiran*'s distinguished status is signalled by its pointed roof; all the other buildings have hipped roofs, except for the family shrines and the *meru* towers.

Other Royal Family Members
To the east of the most central court lies the *saren kangin*, the residential quarters for royalty not in the ruler's immediate family—usually an older branch of the incumbent royal family. The basic layout of the *saren kangin* resembles the typical residential compound, arranged around a central *natar*, with family shrines in the *kaja-kangin* corner, an *umah meten* to the west of this and a *bale gede* to the east. The western counterpart of the *saren kangin* is the *saren kauh*, where junior members of the royal family live— for example, the raja's younger brother.

Variations on a Theme
The picture given here is idealised; actual palaces can differ greatly from the archetypal plan. Alterations mean that over time palace complexes can sprawl as new courtyards are added and walls removed, and even the basic orientations may be modified. In Bangli, for example, the principal palace is situated in the *kaja-kelod* sector, which means that the main entrance is on the eastern side of the complex, rather than the west where it should ideally be.

Prince or Commoner?
Not much distinguishes the palace of a raja or Balinese prince from the residential compounds of his former subjects. The main difference is their overall size, the quality of the building materials and the degree of ornamentation. Gateways, standing on the threshold of the royal precincts, provide an opportunity for impressive display of sculptured forms and other decorative elements.

Floating Pavilion
The *bale kambang* at the
royal palace of Klungkung
(above) was built as
recently as the 1940s but
nevertheless conforms to
the archetypal design of a
floating pavilion, surrounded by water with access
across a causeway.

Water Pavilions

Ornate Pillar Base
The base of a pillar from
the pavilion at Klungkung.

Water pavilions, or 'floating palaces'
(*bale kambang*) as they are more
poetically known, occupy a special
place in Balinese architecture.

Traditionally, the garden of the
ruler in Java during the Hindu-
Buddhist era seems to have been
perceived in a mystical light—a
place apart from the mundane
world where the king could go to
meditate and commune with the
gods. An island at the centre of a
lake or pond appears to have been a
typical feature.

This design may have originated
in cosmographical terms as a
representation of the Hindu-
Buddhist universe with the ruler
positioned at the centre, his
temporal powers sanctioned by
the gods.

Similar ideas existed in Bali. The
temple complex at Taman Ayun in
the former kingdom of Mengwi is
completely surrounded by a moat
and was built as an earthly replica of
the heavens where the deified ancestors of the royal family of Mengwi
are supposed to disport themselves in
floating pavilions attended to by
celestial nymphs—a delightful idea
and one that was replicated in the
ornamental lotus pools and *bale
kambang* of Balinese palaces.

The Canadian-born composer and
writer Colin McPhee, who lived in
Bali for several years before the
Second World War, provides this
atmospheric description in *A House
in Bali* of his visits to the water
garden in the palace compound of
the impoverished Raja of Saba, in

the former kingdom of Karangasem: "As our friendship grew the Anak Agung's gifts (without which I could never depart) became more personal —a ring; a handsome fighting cock; a cutting from one of his precious litchi trees. And always three or four *gurami* fish fresh from the water, still twitching on the thong that held them by the gills.

"These fish were fat and delicious, and were raised in an artificial pond that lay in the park beyond the palace. Once this had been a fine garden, but now hibiscus, gardenia, jasmine and poinsettia fought amongst themselves beneath the confusion of palms. Orchids drooped from boughs, and the ground was black and slippery. The pond had a little pleasure pavilion in the centre, connected to the land by a rickety bamboo bridge, and here the Anak Agung often took his siesta, alone or accompanied."

McPhee became a firm friend of Anak Agung Bagus and was a frequent guest at the palace: "...after we had eaten, I would walk through the park to the pavilion in the pond, which was given to me each time I came. Surrounded by water in this forgotten park, in this far island of friendly and mysterious people—this seemed the final exquisite isolation. In the stillness two turtle-doves called and answered monotonously, I read until I fell asleep."

Certain Balinese floating pavilions are also places of major historical interest. The *bale kambang* in front of the old palace at Kerta Gosa, the island's former centre of justice, was the site for a mass ritual suicide (known as the *puputan*, or ending) during violent conflict with the Dutch colonialists in 1908.

Taman Ujung

The complex of pools and pavilions at Taman Ujung was built by the last ruler of Karangasem, Anak Agung Angulurah Ketut, and was one of three water palaces that he built during his lifetime, the other two being at Tirtaganagga and Jungutan. Most of the standing structures were destroyed during the eruption of Gunung Agung and by subsequent seismic activity but the limpid pools and lotus blossoms remain. What does survive of the pavilions that once overlooked them would seem to indicate a rather vulgar appropriation of Western neo-Classical architecture so perhaps their destruction was no great loss.

Bali Aga Architecture

The Bali Aga House

The Bali Aga house is a rectangular post and beam structure supporting a steeply pitched roof made of bamboo shingles or a thick grass thatch. It is raised on a low plinth of compacted earth, faced with stone, and the walls are typically thick wooden planks or plaited bamboo strips. The windows, if they occur at all, are small. A single door faces the centre of the compound. Like the lowland Balinese, house dimensions are based on bodily measurements taken from the male head of the household. One feature that distinguishes Bali Aga architecture from that of the lowland is the division of the interior of the house into male and female spaces. The uphill (*kaja*) end of the house is for men —it is where they sit when they are inside—while women are linked with the downhill (*kelod*) end of the house, where food is prepared and stored.

The people who live in the mountains of central Bali are rather different from other Balinese. It is often implied that they represent a kind of ancestral population—what the Balinese were like before the arrival of Hindu and Buddhist influences from India and Java.

This is really not the case and many of the Bali Aga's cultural traditions are clearly related to those of their lowland cousins.

Nevertheless, they do constitute a distinct population in their own right and have exercised an independent existence since the earliest times— many of the edicts of the first Hindu-Buddhist kings of Bali, in the 10th century, were addressed to the village communities that are today classified as Bali Aga.

The principal point of divergence between lowland and mountain Balinese seems to have been the resistance of the latter to Majapahit influences from the 14th century onwards: the Bali Aga people do not cremate their dead, they are not organised into castes, and so forth. Naturally their remote location in the mountains has played a big part

in helping the Bali Aga to retain their cultural and political autonomy.

This isolation has also meant that they have retained more of their Austronesian cultural heritage than their lowland neighbours, who came under the influence of the Hindu courts established by Javanese prices and Majapahit settlers.

This helps to explain, if not justify, the tendency to represent the Bali Aga as a kind of aboriginal population.

Village Layout

The Bali Aga villages are spatially oriented along the same lines as those in the lowlands, being laid out in relation to a mountain-sea axis (*kaja-kelod*) and the path of the sun. In other respects, however, they are quite different.

In the first place, although the Bali Aga live in extended family compounds, individual structures within the compound are not functionally differentiated and each building constitutes a self-contained unit which is home to a married couple, their children and the odd elderly parent.

These quite separate households are called *kuren*, which is the common term for both a hearth and the group of people who share the food cooked on it. *Kuren* represent the basic social and economic unit of Bali Aga society.

Compound Layout

As far as the layout of the compound is concerned, the individual houses are arranged in rows along an uphill-downhill axis, with the most senior member of the extended family occupying the house at the uphill (*kaja*) end of the compound. As the male children of a couple marry and

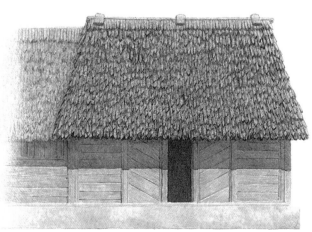

The Bale Agung

A distinctive feature of Bali Aga society is the council of elders, which presides over community affairs. Its members are the most senior married men in the village. When a member dies or steps down, his place is taken by his eldest married son or the next youngest married man in the village. The village council meets periodically to discuss community affairs and each village has a great hall (or *bale agung*) where they assemble. This is an elongated structure rather like an open-sided cattle shed but raised on a masonry plinth. Council members sit according to their status in the community, with the most senior members at the uphill (*kaja*) end of the building. In the same way that residence patterns within the family compound reflect the relative status of the individual households, the overall seating plan in the *bale agung* quite literally maps out the local social hierarchy on the ground.

form their own households, new houses are added at the downhill end of the row.

At the same time, however, as older generations die, the houses they occupied at the uphill end become vacant and are inherited by younger couples, rather like a game of musical chairs. In this respect, residence patterns within the compound reflect the relative status of different household within the extended family group.

Sometimes one finds two rows of houses laid out in parallel within a single compound, which indicates that the compound was established by more than one founder—by a pair of brothers, for example.

Bali Aga villages, of which a number may be found throughout the mountains around Kintamani, are distinguished by their unusual layout and the uniformity of the houses, as if they all adhere to a single design. However, the traditional Bali Aga architecture is disappearing in many places as houses are rebuilt using modern materials.

Pura Penulisan

The temple complex at Pura Penulisan has been an important centre of Bali Aga worship since earliest times. Perched high (l745 metres) on the ring of mountains that surrounds Gunung Batur, the series of ascending terraces recalls similar prehistoric sites in other parts of the Indonesian archipelago. The earliest inscriptions, written in an ancient Javanese script, date from the 11th century and relate to a number of male and female statues, on the uppermost terrace, generally assumed to be portraits of royalty. Their presence may indicate the existence of an ancestral cult of divine rulers similar to the god-kings (*devarajas*) of Angkor in Cambodia.

Pura Sakawana, Penulisan.

Modern Influences

The advent of mass tourism in the past few decades in Bali has had a considerable impact on the physical appearance of Denpasar, the island's capital, and the principal tourist destinations of Nusa Dua, Kuta, Candi Desa, Lovina and Ubud.

The enormous injection of foreign money into the island's economy, combined with the need to cater for the requirements of these visitors from overseas, has inevitably caused changes to the built environment.

The Bali Beach Hotel at Sanur marked a rather ominous start to the tourist boom, being a singularly unimaginative piece of Modernist architecture in the so-called International style whose eight storeys dominate the skyline of what would otherwise be an idyllic tropical shore. It is hard to imagine a building less in sympathy with the local surroundings, both architectural and natural.

Old Meets New
This Art Deco-style *candi bentar* (split gateway) was built in the 1930s in Banjar Intaran, Sanur.

Fortunately, since the early Seventies, when this excrescence was put up, there has been a conscious attempt to respect the essential character of Balinese architectural style wherever possible. Many international hotels have successfully modelled their chalet-style accommodation on Balinese pavilions, albeit with a few extra facilities thrown in such as running water and air-conditioning, while other regional forms have also been adopted and adapted to extend the range of building types in Bali. The layout and landscaping of the Bali Hilton, at Nusa Dua, for example,

recalls the Javanese palace or *kraton*, while the Indies-style architecture of the colonial era provides a historical precedent for an imaginative synthesis of Indonesian and European architectural traditions.

Of course, the appropriation and the manipulation of local forms for new applications runs the risk of trivialising or otherwise corrupting traditional architectural values—the inappropriate use of temple structures is a case in point—and it is important for architects and developers to consult Balinese building experts (*udangi*) when planning a new project. At the same time, the incorporation of local elements as adornment for structures that would otherwise be entirely utilitarian or functional encourages the tendency towards pastiche, which similarly devalues local architectural traditions. Both these tendencies are evident in Bali.

Fortunately, there are also a great many instances of truly inspired designs that incorporate the best of traditional Balinese architecture. The Amankila Hotel in Karangasem, for example, with its limpid pools and colonnades, is clearly modelled on the idea of a traditional Balinese water garden. In this instance, the lily ponds and floating pavilions are entirely in keeping with the pursuit of leisure and relaxation, recalling the enthusiasms of the last ruler of Karangasem who was responsible for building three such complexes at Taman Ujung, Tirtaganagga and Jungutan.

Compound Layout
The massive expansion of tourist shopping facilities in recent years has seen the development of a new type

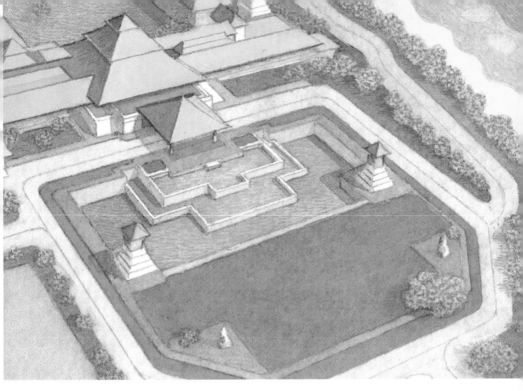

of building in the Balinese architectural repertoire, the shophouse (*ruko*). Clearly modelled on the traditional Chinese shophouse found in every Indonesian town and indeed all over Southeast Asia, the *ruko* (the word is a conflation of *rumah*, meaning house, and *toko*, or shop) is nonetheless a very Balinese creation.

One distinctive feature of the *ruko* is the location of the family temple (*sanggah*) on the roof. This seemingly incongruous marriage of the old and the new actually makes perfect sense in terms of traditional Balinese architectural principles, which require that the *sanggah* occupy the highest level in the domestic compound.

Blending Styles

The Bali Hilton, Nusa Dua, represents a synthesis of Javanese and Balinese architectural traditions with a dash of Dutch colonial thrown in for good measure. The large lawn in front is reminiscent of the grass court (*alun alun*) in front of Javanese palaces (*kraton*)—for example, those at Yogyakarta and Surakarta—while the high roof of the main lobby area recalls a Javanese-style *pendapa* pavilion or its close Balinese relative, the *wantilan*.

A typical modern shophouse (*ruko*) in Bali, with the family temple—and satellite dish—on the roof. The side walls are left windowless in the anticipation that someone will build on the adjacent site to create a terrace of similar shophouses.

Bibliography

Budihardjo, Eko   1986 *Architectural Conservation in Bali.* Gadjah Muda University Press.

Covarrubias, Miguel   1937 *The Island of Bali.* Oxford University Press reprint [1972].

Eiseman, Fred   1990 *Bali Sekala & Niskala* (2 volumes). Hong Kong: Periplus Editions.

Hobart, Angela, Urs Ramseyer & Albert Leemann   1996 *The Peoples of Bali.* Oxford: Blackwells Publishers Ltd.

Hobart, Mark   1978 'The Path of the Soul: The Legitimacy of Nature in Balinese Conceptions of Space', in G. Milner (ed.), *Natural Symbols in South-East Asia.* London: School of Oriental and African Studies.

Howe, L.   1983 'An Introduction to the Cultural Study of Traditional Balinese Architecture'. *Archipel* 25:137-58.

Kempers, Bernet   1991 *Monumental Bali: Introduction to Balinese Archaeology & Guide to the Monuments.* Singapore: Periplus Editions.

Soebadio, H.   1975 'The Documentary Study of Traditional Balinese Architecture: Some Preliminary Notes'. *Indonesian Quarterly* 3:86-95.

Swellengrebel, J.L.   1947 *Een vorstenwijding op Bali.* Leiden.

Tan, R.   1967 'The Domestic Architecture of South Bali'. *Bijdragen tot de Taal-, Land- en Volkenkunde* 123 (4):442-75.